− 6 NOV 2013

4/12/13

31/12/13

4/2/14

HAMPSHIRE COUNTY LIBRARY

WITHDRAWN

Get **more** out of libraries

Please return or renew this item by the last date shown.

You can renew online at www.hants.gov.uk/library

Or by phoning 0845 603 5631

Hampshire
County Council

D0512447

C014682356

's Guide

Hampshire County Library	
C014682356	
Askews	Jul-2010
373	£9.99
	9781861440938

First published in Great Britain in 2010 by
Need2Know
Remus House
Coltsfoot Drive
Peterborough
PE2 9JX
Telephone 01733 898103
Fax 01733 313524
www.need2knowbooks.co.uk

Need2Know is an imprint of Forward Press Ltd.
www.forwardpress.co.uk
All Rights Reserved
© Glynis Kozma 2010
SB ISBN 978-1-86144-093-8
Cover photograph: Dreamstime

Contents

Introduction

This book aims to help you as a parent choose the right secondary school and be prepared for the new situations your child is likely to encounter during their school years.

As a parent you will want to choose the best school for your child. You will want to know whether a state school or an independent school is better and how to make the right choice between any of the schools you are considering. The choices can be difficult as everyone you speak to will have a different opinion.

When your child starts secondary school, it is a major stage in both your lives; gone is the familiarity of primary school and the other parents you knew at the school gate. In its place is a larger school, possibly a greater distance away and with a much broader curriculum.

Since you were at school, there will have been many changes in what is studied, and how. Understanding the curriculum can be a challenge, as there are new subjects which have appeared and some subjects that are the same but now have a different name. All of this can make the secondary school curriculum quite daunting.

Although most children settle into their new schools well, teething troubles can occur, as well as other problems connected to friendships or academic work. It can be hard to know when to intervene and when to step back and allow your child to fend for themselves.

Every parent wants their child to fulfil their potential academically and form happy relationships within the school environment. Knowing what approach to take when problems arise can make all the difference between something being smoothed over quickly or becoming a bigger problem.

This book takes you through the process of choosing a school, the first day, common problems, examinations and options for children after GCSEs. Further help and support can be found in the help list.

The secondary school process does not need to be stressful – this book is here to help.

Disclaimer

All the information and dates contained in this book are correct at the time of going to press. Please see the government resources in the help list for the most up-to-date information regarding the National Curriculum, GCSEs, AS and A Levels.

Acronyms

A Level	Advanced Level
ADD	attention deficit disorder
ADHD	attention deficit and hyperactivity disorder
ASD	autistic spectrum disorder
AS Level	Advanced Subsidiary Level
BTEC	Business and Technical Education Council
FS	foundation stage
GCSE	General Certificate in Secondary Education
ICT	information and communication technology
IEP	Individual Education Plan
KS1	Key Stage 1 (Years 1-2)
KS2	Key Stage 2 (Years 3-6)
KS3	Key Stage 3 (Years 7-9)
KS4	Key Stage 4 (Years 10-11)
KS5	Key Stage 5 (Age 16-18)
LA	local authority
NVQ	National Vocational Qualification
Ofsted	Office of Standards in Education, Children's Services and Skills
PE	physical education
PSHE	personal, social and health education
QCDA	Qualifications and Curriculum Development Agency
RE	religious education
SATs	Statutory Assessment Tests
SENCO	special educational needs co-ordinator
SENDIST	Special Educational Needs and Disability Tribunal
SpLD	specific learning difficulty
UCAS	Universities and Colleges Admission Services

Chapter One

Choosing a School

You have no sooner got used to coping with primary school when, suddenly, your children are off to secondary school. Starting secondary school is a major step in a child's life. Compared with the cosiness and familiarity of primary school, where they've waited at the gate at home time, it's a whole new educational world.

For some parents, choice is not an issue. You may only have one school on the doorstep, or catchment area rules mean that you cannot send your child anywhere else. But if you do have a choice of secondary schools, it can be a difficult decision. Conflicting opinions from friends and other parents don't help and can make the choice all that more difficult.

However, there is more to choosing a school than just listening to other parents and going along to an open day, but where do you start?

'There is more to choosing a school than just listening to other parents and going along to an open day.'

Independent school

Most independent schools' day fees are in the region of £10,000 a year. This could, of course, be less, but it could also be much more if your child is a boarder. If fees are not an issue, how do you decide whether to opt for the independent sector? Here are the key differences:

- Classes tend to be smaller.

- Independent schools do not have to follow the National Curriculum.

- Facilities may be better, e.g. on-site swimming pool, drama theatre or choice of musical tuition.

- Pastoral care for students will be provided by house staff who are responsible for day or boarding pupils.

- Depending on your own views, the ethos of a particular independent school may be important.

Class size is a very important factor. This tends to be what you pay for, along with better equipment and buildings. Compared with average class sizes of 30 pupils in the state sector, independent schools could have 8-20 pupils in a class, meaning your child should receive more individual attention. Although they will be given more time with the teachers, they may also be expected to perform at a higher level as a result of this.

Independent schools don't have to follow the National Curriculum, so you could find they offer a totally different learning experience. Some independent schools have a very strong identity, and this might influence what they provide and where the emphasis is in the curriculum. For example, they could be a school with a strong history of sport, music or drama. It is vital that you take this into account when choosing what will be appropriate for your child. Some children could be very unhappy at a school because they don't play certain sports well and there is nothing else on offer.

The decision between the independent and state sector is not always as straightforward as you might think.

- An excellent state school might serve your child better than an average independent school.

- An average child might flounder at a highly academic independent school, whereas they might be very happy at a good state school.

- An average child might respond well to the extra attention and small classes at an independent school which does not focus solely on academic success but encourages pupils to develop all their talents.

Keep an open mind. If you can afford an independent education for your child, don't dismiss your local state schools outright – they might be excellent. Be aware of what is on offer and look at all schools in your area before you make your final decision. And, as with any school, look at:

- The quality of exam results.

- The overall educational values of the school.

- Pastoral care, such as on-site counsellors or access to counselling.

- The head teacher and leaders at the school, are they established or new to the school?

- What opportunities can the school offer your child?

- What is the main destination of leavers – college, university or employment?

State school

If your child is one of the 93% of children who attend state schools, you'll want to know what to look for in the state schools on your doorstep.

In some counties you will not have a choice. Admissions criteria to secondary schools can change and your child may be sent to the secondary school that is nearest, or that accepts children from a pool of feeder primary schools – or both. If you are a parent whose child's secondary school is decided by your postcode, then having a preference is not an option – unless you appeal against the decision of your local authority (LA) (this is covered later on in this chapter).

State schools fall into two broad groups:

- Non-selective.

- Selective.

The majority of state schools are non-selective, meaning that your child will not have to sit an entrance examination. Some selective state schools may be classed as grammar schools and pupils will have to sit an 11-plus type of entrance exam, or the school's own entrance exam, before being awarded a place. Grammar schools are few and far between in the UK, and if your child has the option of a grammar school education, you will need to weigh up the benefits as you would with any school.

Make sure you know which secondary schools your child is eligible for – there is no point spending time looking at schools if you live outside their catchment area, and it's not unusual for parents to have decided on a particular school only to find that the admission rules have changed. If you have lived in your area for some time, you will probably know which schools you can apply to, but if you are new to the area, you might have to contact your LA's education department to find out.

Researching your local schools

League tables

There is a lot you can find out about a school before you even set foot in it. First, there are league tables now called 'School and College Achievement and Attainment Tables'. Visit www.dscf.gov.uk and click 'school performance tables' to find your local area's league tables.

These tables show the performance of a school in relation to other schools in your area. You can find out how many children achieved five A-C grade GCSEs at a school in any one year. You will also find the number of children who took those exams and how the grades compared with previous years, and the county average will also be listed. However, apart from facts and figures, league tables don't tell you much more. They can't tell you anything about the yearly intake, which could have an affect on exam results – e.g. an influx of very bright pupils one year could give the impression of a school being better than it is, and vice versa.

League tables group state and independent schools' results together – so be careful not to make the mistake of comparing a selective independent school with a non-selective state school as this won't be a fair comparison.

It is important to look back over a number of years to see if there is pattern to the results. By looking at the results from several years, you can spot if a school is in decline, if the results are lower every year, or if they are an improving school with results getting better each year.

You also need to look at the UK average for results as this will give you more of a picture of just how your local schools are performing. Schools have to include passes at A-C grade for both English and maths. How a school performs at these basic subjects tells you more about it than how many A-C passes they have in drama or PE.

'There is a lot you can find out about a school before you even set foot in it. First, there are league tables now called "School and College Achievement and Attainment Tables".'

Ofsted reports

If teachers hate league tables, then they hate Ofsted inspections even more!

An Ofsted (Office for Standards in Education) report is the result of an inspection that the school has every four to five years. The report covers many different aspects of school life, including the teaching quality in each subject, the management of the school and the overall ethos of the school. You can find reports for your local schools on Ofsted's website (see help list). Alternatively, your local library should have copies of reports on local schools.

Many parents find Ofsted reports rather daunting and full of jargon. The reports are summarised and the essential parts to look for are:

- The overall grade – this will be 'excellent', 'good' or 'satisfactory'.

- Summary – this states very concisely what the inspectors have found with regard to leadership, management, quality of teaching, communication with parents and pupil achievement.

- Recommendations – these are what the school has to improve upon. This part of the inspection highlights any weaknesses, including the teaching of a subject, leadership, facilities, and so on.

There are reports on each subject and the management of the school. These will usually say if the head is effective and how the senior management team works. Look at the recommendations to see what the school has to do to be better. Many schools have a rather bland report – not too good, but not too bad, but if you read the recommendations, this will give you more of an insight. If your child has special needs, you should look at the provision for this.

You could have a look at the previous inspection and compare any changes. If the school has had a change of head teacher, what direction is the school going in now? Up, down or no change? The report can be helpful but is only part of what you need to consider when researching which secondary school to choose.

Prospectus and website

A school's prospectus and/or website can give you some basic information about the school, like how big it is, what facilities are available and what clubs and activities are run there.

Prospectuses are usually available at the open day of the school, but you should be able to get a copy at any time by contacting the school or downloading it from their website.

You should bear in mind that an impressive website and prospectus does not necessarily mean the school is good. Equally, an out-of-date website or poorly designed prospectus is not necessarily an indication that a school is bad. Some schools may spend more on PR.

Other parents

This is where you may become very confused! There is no denying that all parents sound-out other parents about which school to send their child to. Almost everything you hear from other parents will be a matter of personal opinion. Try to speak to parents whose children are currently attending the school to ensure what you hear is up-to-date information. Myths about a school's reputation can hang around for years after they have ceased to be true, so be cautious about taking everything on board.

Visiting an independent school

The earlier you visit the school, the better. Many popular schools will be heavily over-subscribed, so the sooner you put your child's name on the list, the better. If you are reading this and have Eton in mind, you are probably too late!

It depends too on whether your child attends an independent preparatory school or a state primary school. If you are already in the independent system, you need to consider when your child will move to secondary school – usually after Year 8 when they have taken their Common Entrance exam. However, if you are moving into the state sector for secondary education, your child will transfer at the end of Year 6.

'You should bear in mind that an impressive website and prospectus does not necessarily mean the school is good. Equally, an out-of-date website or poorly designed prospectus is not necessarily an indication that a school is bad.'

There is a lot of information available about independent schools. *The Good Schools Guide* (Lucas Publications) gives plenty of information, but there is no substitute for visiting and asking your own questions.

Visiting a state school

School visits are arranged just under a year before your child begins secondary school – this means the October before the September when your child is due to start.

- Visit your chosen schools during October.
- Complete your applications by the end of October.
- Receive an offer of a place by March the following year.
- Make a decision to accept or appeal against the decision. You will usually have around two weeks to accept, or start the appeal process by the end of the month. Check your LA's website for detailed information on the deadlines for this.
- Your child will begin their new school in September.

Essentially, this means you will only visit the school once before deciding whether to send your child there. If you want to begin looking earlier so you have a better idea of your choices, bear the following in mind.

The advantages of looking earlier include:

- You can look at schools twice to get a clearer picture of what they offer.
- You will have more time to make further enquiries before making your decision.
- You can monitor the school's exam results over two years.
- You will avoid a frantic couple of weeks when you might be visiting several schools.

The disadvantages of looking earlier include:

- Schools and staff change. A change of head teacher can make a huge difference.

- Admissions criteria can change and you may not be eligible for certain schools in another year's time.

What to look for when you visit

Accept that open days are set-pieces. The school undergoes a mammoth clean-up, the pupils are under strict instructions to behave well at all times, lessons are prepared extra carefully and the head teacher tries to convince you at all costs that their school is the only one worth sending your child to.

'There are many excellent schools which are in desperate need of refurbishment – so don't be too put off if the walls need a lick of paint. However, litter and obvious signs of graffiti that have not been dealt with are definite turn-offs.'

There are many excellent schools which are in desperate need of refurbishment – so don't be too put off if the walls need a lick of paint. However, litter and obvious signs of graffiti that have not been dealt with are definite turn-offs. If you are visiting outside of an arranged open day, you might well get a real picture of what the school is like.

It's good to have some questions prepared in advance to ask the head teacher. Some examples could be:

- What approach does the school take on discipline?
- How often is homework set and in what quantity?
- On what basis are children in sets or streamed – Year 6 SATs or a teacher's report?
- Are they in sets for all subjects or just the core subjects – English, maths and science?
- How easy is it to move sets or streams?
- What are the arrangements for lunch times? Are pupils allowed to go home or into town? What is the lunch menu like – are there healthy options?
- What about the pastoral care? Is there a mentoring scheme operating at the school?
- What after-school clubs and activities exist at the school?
- What sports are offered and what is equipment like?
- What subject choices are available at GCSE and A Level?

- Which subjects are compulsory and which languages are on offer?

Your child's opinion

Do take your child's opinion into account; talk to them about each school you are considering and discuss the pros and cons of each. Many children will want to go to the same school as their existing group of friends, making the issue quite emotionally charged if you would prefer them to go to a different school. The important thing is to be open and honest with your child.

Admissions criteria

As the admissions criteria changes from year to year, the best place to access information is from the booklet given to you when your child is in Year 6. Another good place to find out about the admissions criteria in your local area is from your LA's website.

How do I apply?

If you are applying to an independent secondary school, you should contact the school and follow their procedure for admission. If you are applying to a state school and your child is not at a state primary school, you should apply at the same time as children in Year 6 currently attending state schools, and if your child is already in Year 6 at a state school, you will be guided through the transfer to secondary school by the school.

If your child currently attends a state primary school in the UK, the application form will be given to you either by your child's school or it will come from your LA by post. Some LAs will allow you to apply online, so check with your LA if they offer this option. If your child is not at a state school and has, for instance, attended an independent primary school or a school outside the UK, you should contact your LA to request a form as you will not be sent one automatically.

'Do take your child's opinion into account; talk to them about each school you are considering and discuss the pros and cons of each.'

The application form is very simple. All you need to include is your name, address, details of your child and the schools you want to apply to; usually you can list up to three schools in order of preference. It is important that you return the form by the date required, which is usually by the end of October or beginning of November preceding transfer to secondary school the following September. The deadline will vary each year, but your LA will inform you.

Once you've submitted your application form, you will then receive a letter giving you your child's allocated school and also the option to return a slip to say whether you accept or refuse that school. If you refuse the school which is allocated, you will then start the appeal process which follows a set format and has deadlines. You usually have around two weeks to accept or decline the place.

Appealing a decision

If you apply for a place at a state secondary school and are not give the school of your choice, you have the right to appeal against the decision.

In order to appeal, you need to follow the procedure set out by your LA. Each LA has their own appeal procedure, so before you start the appeal process look online for guidance. The first step will be to meet the deadline for the appeal, by completing the relevant forms. You should visit your LA's website or speak to their education department on the phone to find out when the deadline is and request a copy of the form.

You may also write a letter of appeal to accompany the appeal form, giving further reasons why you want your child to attend that school. This gives you the opportunity to support your case.

Your appeal will be heard by a panel made up of three members of the public. This panel is chosen according to legal guidelines and does not, for example, include school governors. The panel members have to receive training. The meeting is formal but friendly and you will not need a lawyer. The panel will usually sit at a table and you will sit on the other side. You are then asked to present your case in accordance with the reasons stated in your letter of appeal.

Prior to meeting with you, the panel will meet with the school and the school will prove that they followed the School Admissions Code. If it is found that they have followed this, you will be given a chance to present a counter-argument to the panel.

- Explain why you believe that the school would be the best place for your child.

- Tell the panel about any special circumstances that might justify your child being awarded a place.

- Submit additional evidence or documentation that might be relevant to your appeal, like a medical note from a doctor to support an application on the basis of a social or medical need.

The panel's decision is binding and can only be overturned in court. You can, however, contact your Local Government Ombudsman (www.lgo.org.uk). They can recommend a new appeal, but they cannot overturn the previous decision. The time between submitting your appeal and finding out whether it has been successful can be as long as three months.

In the meantime, you can put your child's name on the school's list of 'continuing interest'. This means that if a child leaves or does not take up their place, your child will be considered for a place along with others on the list.

More information about the appeal process can be found on www.directgov.uk, the Children's Legal Centre: www.childrenslegalcentre.com and from the Advisory Centre for Education: www.ace-ed.org.uk.

Summing Up

- Start looking at schools when your child is in Year 5 or sooner.

- Ensure that you know which secondary schools your child is eligible for.

- Research your local schools by using lots of different sources of information to help you make your decision about your preferred school.

- Make sure that you keep to the application deadline.

Chapter Two

Special Needs

Children who have special needs are encouraged to be taught in a mainstream school as far as possible. Special educational needs (SEN) are catered for through the SEN Code of Practice. This gives guidance on how children are identified as having a special educational need and how it can be met.

Special educational needs apply to a child who has difficulty learning at the same rate as their peers, or who has a disability. Special needs can include:

- Dyslexia.

- Dyspraxia.

- Asperger's syndrome.

- Autistic spectrum disorders.

- ADHD/ADD.

- A physical disability.

- Learning difficulties.

- Behavioural difficulties.

- Sensory impairment.

- Gifted and talented.

Your child's school will have a special needs policy devised by the governing body and the head teacher. Day-to-day implementation of this will be through the special educational needs co-ordinator (SENCO). The SENCO will have responsibility for the children with special educational needs in the classroom setting. The governing body decides how much of the budget is allocated to special needs provision and what form that provision takes.

If your child was identified as having special needs at primary school, details of these will be sent to their secondary school. If your child had a Statement of Special Educational Needs then funding for this should follow your child to their new school. If you child doesn't have this then it's recommended that you speak with the school's SENCO about what provisions they could offer your child. You should do this prior to making your final decision on which is your preferred choice of school.

Very few children now have statements. Most children who have special needs receive support at two levels:

- School Action – this is where your child's needs are identified and support is provided by the school. This may or may not include additional one-to-one support or differentiation.

- School Action Plus – this is where your child's needs are identified and the school provides support from a team of people over and above teachers in school. These other people will come into school to support your child or advise the school.

Individual Education Plans

All children who have special needs should have an Individual Education Plan (IEP). This plan identifies needs, sets short- and longer-term goals and suggests how these goals can be attained. The goals should be achievable, measurable and realistic. The IEP is usually compiled by the SENCO, in consultation with other teachers and anyone else involved. It is then discussed with you and your child so that you are aware of the targets and any role you might have in helping to achieve them. IEPs tend to be reviewed once a term and amended accordingly. You should be aware that your child has an IEP and ensure that you have seen it and signed it.

Specific learning difficulties

Some learning difficulties are called specific learning difficulties (SpLDs). These include dyslexia and dyspraxia. As well as having problems with literacy, numeracy and co-ordination, these children may also find it hard to

'If your child was identified as having special needs at primary school, details of these will be sent to their secondary school. If your child had a Statement of Special Educational Needs then funding for this should follow your child to their new school.'

concentrate, have difficulty with handwriting or sports, are disorganised and forgetful, and develop low self-esteem or behavioural problems. They do have strengths too, often in art, computing and design.

If your child has an SpLD, you need to ensure that all their teachers are aware of it. A whole-school approach works best, but it occasionally happens that important information does not reach all teachers. This is likely if, for example, your child has a change of teacher throughout the same academic year. If you think that your child's teachers are not aware of your child's needs, you can either write to or request a meeting with the SENCO, your child's form tutor or year head.

What help is there for children with SpLDs?

Provision for children with SpLDs varies enormously between schools, as well as between independent and state schools. Some LAs have specialist units for children with dyslexia, but these are very few and far between.

Your child may have individual or small group tuition with a specialist teacher through the school. This could be once a week or more, and your child will be withdrawn from lessons to have this help. Sometimes independent schools offer tuition as an extra that parents pay for. If your child has an SpLD and you are choosing an independent school, ensure that you understand what they offer and whether it is included in the fees or not.

Provision does vary substantially between schools. Some schools employ specialist teachers who will teach your child one-on-one, but other schools may offer in-class support from a learning support assistant. The size of the learning support department at the school will give you some indication of the amount of support offered.

Independent special schools

If your child has particular special needs, you might want to consider an independent special school; these are independent, day or boarding schools.

Special schools usually have small classes and all teaching takes into account the children's needs. In most cases, all the teachers have additional training and there is a whole-school approach to learning. There is often a high ratio of teachers to pupils, including learning support assistants.

Schools that have a withdrawal system offer children specialist teaching outside of lessons, usually with a specialist teacher.

Gifted and talented children

'Some children have special needs because they are very bright. As a rough guide, children who are in the top 2% of the ability range – that is to say they are brighter than 98% of their peers – are considered as gifted.'

Some children have special needs because they are very bright. As a rough guide, children who are in the top 2% of the ability range – that is to say they are brighter than 98% of their peers – are considered as gifted. If children were grouped throughout school by ability and not age, these children would be two or three years ahead of children the same age as them. You may not think it is a problem to be bright, or that the term 'special needs' would apply.

However, children who are very bright sometimes fail to reach their potential for a number of reasons. These can include:

■ Being bored, so they lose motivation.

■ Not wanting to appear a 'know all' so they hold back and try not to draw attention to themselves, often resulting in under-performing.

■ Becoming badly behaved through boredom, and being labelled a troublemaker.

■ Putting very little effort into their work as they find it too easy, so they rush it and produce results far below their capabilities.

■ Working hard at one or two subjects which hold their interest, but not bothering with other subjects.

Sometimes, gifted children can either tend to become withdrawn or can become badly behaved, but not all gifted children suffer behavioural problems – many adapt well and succeed academically without any problems. Some though may feel isolated and find it hard to make friends. In these instances, it is a good idea to try to meet other families with children in the same situation for mutual support.

Schools have an obligation to meet the needs of gifted pupils in the same way that they have to meet the needs of all children. They should be able to differentiate the work – that is, set your gifted child work that is more demanding.

If you think your child is gifted and undiagnosed, the best route is to have a full educational assessment by an educational psychologist. This currently costs in the region of £400. Once you have this information, you can then decide on the best route for your child – be it another school or the current school making some adaptations and meeting their needs. Bear in mind though that some schools will not accept an independent assessment and are not obliged to act on its findings.

How can you help your child at home?

Children with any kind of learning difficulty have to work much harder than other children just to keep up. This means that your child will be tired at the end of a school day. They might be reluctant to do their homework, either because they are tired or because they find it hard.

Your child will be ready for a snack and a rest before they tackle homework. Children with any kind of learning difficulty benefit from healthy food – as do all children – and you should avoid snacks that give a quick boost of energy followed by a slump. This means choosing slow-release complex carbohydrates rather than refined, sugary foods. After-school snacks might include:

- Savoury sandwiches made with wholegrain bread.
- Yoghurt and a banana.
- Dried fruit such as apricots, figs and dates.
- Flapjacks.
- Hummus and carrot sticks.

Be supportive but resist the temptation to do their work for them. Try to set a routine so that homework is tackled at the same time each day and have a quiet area for them to work in, away from any distractions. For more information on helping your child tackle their homework, see chapter 4.

Negotiating homework

Sometimes teachers will differentiate the homework they give to a child with special needs. So, instead of having 20 spellings to learn, they might give your child only 10. They might ask them to research a topic online rather than writing up notes on it. However, sometimes teachers don't do this and it can cause problems if your child feels swamped with the amount of homework. This can be especially so during Year 7 when your child is settling into a new school with all the additional pressures involved. If you find that your child is struggling with homework, it is worth contacting the school.

What should you do if you are not satisfied with the school?

'Sometimes teachers will differentiate the homework they give to a child with special needs.'

Some parents do occasionally find that their child's needs are not being met within the SEN Code of Practice.

Your first communication should be with your child's form tutor, head of year or SENCO. If you are still not satisfied then you should contact the governing body, in particular the governor who is responsible for special needs. Schools have a legal obligation to meet the needs of their pupils and can be at risk of having to pay compensation in the future if it is proven that they have not met a child's needs. If you cannot resolve the situation with the school, then you can take your case to the Special Educational Needs and Disability Tribunal (SENDIST). However, this should be a last resort.

After-school activities

All children enjoy clubs and sports outside of school. However, it is worth considering whether your child is in danger of suffering from 'overload' by doing too much all of the time. It is usually good to allow children to participate in sports and activities to boost their self-esteem, but if these activities mean that they are too tired or too busy to complete their essential homework, then maybe a rethink is needed. It might be worth keeping after-school activities to a minimum during Year 7 while you see how they cope with the transition to secondary school.

For more information about the issues covered in this chapter, please see *Special Educational Needs – A Parent's Guide* (Need2Know), *Dyslexia and Other Learning Difficulties – A Parent's Guide* (Need2Know), *ADHD – The Essential Guide* (Need2Know), *Asperger's Syndrome – The Essential Guide* (Need2Know) and *Autism – A Parent's Guide* (Need2Know).

Summing Up

- Develop a good partnership and communication with the school's SENCO.

- Find out about your child's new school's special needs policy.

- Ensure your child has a good diet in order to maintain levels of concentration.

- Try not to involve them in too many after-school activities if they find schoolwork tiring.

- Contact support groups for advice and to enable you to meet other parents in a similar situation.

Chapter Three

The First Day

Most children have very mixed feelings about their new school – as an adult you will be only too aware of the mixture of excitement and apprehension that accompanies new beginnings. Before your child starts their new school, there are things that you can do to make that first day a little less daunting.

How you can help

All of us, including children, feel more at ease in a new situation if we feel good about ourselves. Self-esteem is very important for children as they enter secondary school and their teenage years; so when your child does something well, make sure you acknowledge it. When they are struggling with a task, give encouragement and praise for effort, even when the final results are not necessarily what you had hoped for. This can be for things as mundane as helping in the kitchen, playing well with friends in the park or helping out with younger siblings – not just succeeding academically.

The importance of talking

Some parents can paint such a glowing picture of the new school that their child is afraid to mention any misgivings they might have. Make sure your child knows that it is perfectly normal to have mixed feelings about any new situation, and let them know how you felt about your new school at their age. By doing this you will encourage them to talk about their concerns.

'Most children have very mixed feelings about their new school.'

Many children worry about such small things that they are afraid to mention them in case they are laughed at. But these small worries can grow bigger the longer they are stored away – so they need to be brought out into the open. A lot of negative behaviour and thoughts are founded in a child's imagination – if they can discuss their worries, the anxious feelings tend to shrink.

Ask your child:

- What are you looking forward to most?
- What are you not looking forward to?
- Is there anything that you feel very worried about?
- Whatever it is that is worrying you, what is the worst possible outcome?
- If the very worst happened, what would happen next? How would you deal with that?
- How can we make you feel less anxious?

'A lot of negative behaviour and thoughts are founded in a child's imagination – if they can discuss their worries, the anxious feelings tend to shrink.'

The 'what if' and 'then what' example can work well to weaken anxiety and worry about starting a new school. It works by talking through the worst scenario about a child's worries and helps them to understand that the outcome of their feared scenario perhaps wouldn't be so bad as they are imagining.

For example, if your child is terrified of losing their way around the school, they might be feeling, 'What if I lose my way and get separated from my friends'. This fear could grow in their minds until they feel panicky and sick. You have to say, 'Then what…?' This forces them to confront the possible outcomes.

You can then discuss their options which might include: continuing to look for the classroom they need; going to the school office to ask for help; going into another classroom to ask for help; or asking someone they pass in the corridor for help. So by working through the problem, they can see that if the very worst happened, they would not be in a terrible situation.

Rather than dismissing their worries or just saying, 'Oh that's silly, that won't happen', face the issue head-on and discuss the possible outcome – hopefully this will make them a little bit more relaxed about the prospect of beginning the new term.

Friends

Your child might be starting school with their old friends, or they may be the only one from their primary school going to that new school. Whichever one is your child's situation, it is always worth emphasising that a new school is a good place to make new friends. Whilst you can't choose your child's friends, or make those friends for them, you can be welcoming when they find new friends.

It is common for parents to think their child is now quite independent and doesn't need any help, but some children do feel lonely. Encourage them to invite friends home and out for the day, and do all the things you used to do when they were at primary school. They will tell you pretty quickly if they feel you are over-stepping the mark and want to be more independent.

If your child is shy and quiet, they might need some encouragement, so be there for them. If they don't know anyone in their form or their new school, encourage them to seek out other shy or quiet children; schools often have lunchtime clubs which might help your child meet other like-minded children.

The practicalities of the first day

The best way to ensure your child settles in well is to be organised and to plan ahead – try to teach them to do the same. You won't need to be told about naming everything you can lay your hands on as you have most probably been putting a lot of these practical measures in place throughout their primary school years, but just in case, here they are again:

- If your child will be walking to school and it's a new route, do a trial run together.
- If they're going by bus, make sure they'll have enough time to catch it and that they know what to do if they miss it.
- All belongings should be named.
- Pack school bags the night before.
- Make sure your child gets an early night.

'Your child might be starting school with their old friends, or they may be the only one from their primary school going to that new school. Whichever one is your child's situation, it is always worth emphasising that a new school is a good place to make new friends.'

- Be prepared for your child to complain of tummy aches or feeling sick in the morning – this is probably just last minute nerves. Reassure your child that if they are not better once they begin lessons at school, the secretary will be able to phone you.

- Have the school uniform ready, right down to the socks and pants.

- Ensure your child has their dinner money or packed lunch.

- Provide some emergency money – not to be spent!

- If they are allowed to take a mobile phone to school, ensure it has enough credit on it for emergency calls home. Check your school's policy on mobile phones first. Some schools allow them but insist they are turned-off in lessons, others ban them altogether.

- Make sure your child has your home and work numbers – and that school does too.

Your child will feel much more secure and able to cope with the unexpected if they know how they will get to and from school and what to do in an emergency. Many schools issue their own guidelines for travelling to school safely, but back up from home is always good.

After the first day

For many Year 7 children, a new secondary school feels enormous after the cosiness of their primary school. It is huge, it smells odd, the other pupils are so big and push them out of the way, no one knows their name, their uniform has the dreaded 'room for growth' and they feel lost in it as well as the school. They will be tired when they come home. They may not want to go back – ever. This is all normal – try to help your child get over these first few days by talking to them about it.

- What did they enjoy?

- What was difficult?

- What can they do differently the next day to make it easier?

The first day at a new school can be overwhelming for some children – others take to it without any hesitation. If you plan ahead, your child should feel confident as they step out into this new world. The key to this is to bring any worries out into the open, talk them through and make your child feel confident and good about themselves.

Summing Up

- Build up your child's self-esteem by praising them when they make an effort or do something well.

- Encourage your child to talk openly about worries they have about making the change from primary to secondary school.

- Encourage your child to welcome new friends, join extra curricular activity clubs and invite new friends around at the weekend – it will help them to settle in, especially if they're at a different school to their primary school friends.

- Be organised for the first day and make sure your child knows what to do in case of an emergency.

- Encourage your child to be open with you about their feelings once they have started school; the act of just talking over any worries may be enough to make them disappear. If your child really doesn't cope with the transition, speaking openly with them will mean you are informed and can take appropriate action.

Chapter Four

Homework

Parents hate homework because they battle to get their children to do it; children hate it because they just want to do more interesting things – and, rather surprisingly, teachers aren't too keen on it either – they have to chase it up and mark it.

Homework possibly causes more family arguments than any other schooling issue. It simply doesn't go away. When your child is at secondary school, their homework enters a different league. Forget the few minutes a night that they had in Year 6 – this is more serious stuff. Your child could easily have an hour each day in Year 7 – and up to three hours by Year 11.

If there is one word which can sum up how you can help your child with homework, it is 'communication'. Try to communicate both with your child and their teacher regularly about homework. To help your child get used to this change in pace from primary school you could try:

- Establishing a routine when your child first starts secondary school. This will cultivate time-management skills which will stay with them throughout their school years.

- Taking an interest in your child's homework, but be careful not to do it for them or be too critical when checking it.

- Providing a noise-free environment so they can study without the distraction of a TV or other family members.

- Putting a pin board up in their bedroom or workspace so homework reminders can be put in a prominent place.

- Being supportive and encouraging – give them praise for effort as well as results.

'Parents hate homework because they battle to get their children to do it; children hate it because they just want to do more interesting things.'

- Encouraging them to take regular breaks from their work, to get a drink and move away from the workspace – this will keep concentration levels up.

- Keeping a record of your child's coursework deadlines.

No homework – can this be true?

You should be given information about your child's homework and how regular it will be when they start secondary school. This may be through a letter or the school's website, but if you're not sure, you can always enquire with your child's head of year or form tutor. Most pupils will be given two subjects' homework every night and all pupils will have a homework diary that can be easily checked. The amount of homework will vary from lesson to lesson, but you could expect your child to spend roughly half an hour on each subject in Year 7. By the time they are in Years 10 and 11, they could be spending an hour or more on each subject, amounting to three hours each evening. However, each school has its own policy regarding homework and the quantity they give.

If your child avoids doing homework, it's important to ask the question 'why?' Are they unhappy in school? Are they finding the work too hard? Are they too tired? Try to build a culture of speaking openly with your child so that any problems can be sorted out before they get out of hand.

Coursework

In Years 10 and 11 your child will be asked to complete coursework for some of their GCSE subjects. The rules governing this are constantly changing and they may in future have to complete much of it at school.

The coursework will usually be set so that pupils carry it out over two or three terms and hand in a large final project by the deadline set by their teacher. When the time comes, try to make a note of the deadline; teenagers can be forgetful, and during their GCSE years they are taking so many subjects, several of them requiring coursework to be completed. Try to encourage your child to work on the coursework in bitesize chunks over the time allocated; it's not advisable for students to leave it till the night before the deadline to complete it.

If your child is vague about coursework, you can always contact the school. They will have the dates for completing it.

How much help should I give?

As a parent you will want to help your child if they are stuck with their homework. Children can learn a lot at home with a supportive parent, and it can also boost their confidence enormously. However, problems can occur if your child becomes dependent on your help.

You will need to monitor the situation. If your child becomes constantly out of their depth with a subject, they could be in the wrong set. Or, they could have a teacher who doesn't spend enough time explaining what is required. Alternatively, your child may be inattentive in lessons – though they aren't going to admit that to you! It is best to try to find out as much as you can.

If your child starts to regularly struggle with their homework, ask them:

- Is anyone else in your group finding the homework hard?
- Did your teacher say you might find it difficult?
- Have you explained to your teacher that you find it hard?

Most teachers prefer their pupils to admit that they can't do a piece of work that's been set rather than rely on parental help, unless that parental help is given only occasionally. Your role as a parent is to instil in your child the confidence so that they can ask their teacher for help. Many children are afraid to do so, assuming that they should be able to pick up a new topic immediately. Try to reassure your child that it's okay to ask their teacher for help.

So, help your child now and again, but if they seem to be completely out of their depth, it's a topic for the next parents' night, or sooner if your child is unhappy. Contact the school and ask for a meeting with the relevant teachers.

'Most teachers prefer their pupils to admit that they can't do a piece of work that's been set rather than rely on parental help, unless that parental help is given only occasionally.'

Too much homework

There are two points here. You will need to establish if your child is finding the work itself too difficult, or if they are being given a huge quantity. If you think your child is being given too much homework, establish whether it's for one subject in particular and perhaps even speak to that teacher about it.

If the content is too difficult, again, communication with the school is needed. You should not panic, but if your child is tearful or relies on you to do the work over several weeks then a meeting with the school would be a good idea.

'Your attitude to homework will influence your child enormously, so try to instil motivation and establish a routine for your child.'

Forgotten homework

It can be very demoralising for a child to be in trouble for forgetting their homework, or producing sub-standard work. They end up in teachers' bad books, detention, or both. Your attitude to homework will influence your child enormously, so try to instil motivation and establish a routine for your child, as discussed earlier in this chapter.

Homework not being marked

Teachers usually hate homework, but they have to set it, follow it up and mark it. Sometimes homework that is set is in preparation for the lesson, in this case it won't really need marking as it's quite often a 'thinking' or reading type of homework. However, if you find lengthy exercises are not marked and no feedback is given by your child's teacher, it will be advisable to contact that teacher, or bring it up at a parents' evening.

Summing Up

- Try to establish a routine and teach your child time management skills from early on.

- Provide a workspace and limit distractions while your child is completing their homework or coursework.

- Encourage them to take breaks while they're doing their homework to keep concentration levels up.

- Keep coursework and homework deadlines in a prominent place so your child is reminded of when and what has to be handed in.

- Keep an eye on how much help you give to your child, and don't let it become too regular if possible.

Chapter Five

Friendships

When your child starts their new school, they will probably have some friends who are starting secondary school with them, but they might not know anyone else. It is likely that your child will make friends and settle in quite quickly, but it can be a worry that they will struggle. Try to be relaxed about the prospects of your child's new friendships – they are going through a big transition and need to feel secure within their home environment. Children of this age are still discovering themselves and finding out who they are. You may notice their friendships changing, and they may settle in to a completely new group of friends that doesn't include any of their primary school friends quite soon after starting secondary school.

We all want to see our children blossom, so how can you help them make the most of their secondary school years regarding friendships and socialising?

Your child's friendships and personality

Some children are naturally introverted, and you may be too, so you'll know how they feel. If your child is more inclined to show some of the following behaviours, you should try not to push them too hard into being sociable beyond their comfort zone – as long as they have some friends and are happy, it shouldn't be seen as a problem.

- They might have a few close friends and not really enjoy being part of a loud, noisy group.

- They might tend to hang back at big social gatherings, rather than diving in and talking to strangers.

- They don't need a lot of social interaction and can feel tired if they are with other people too much.

'Children of this age are still discovering themselves and finding out who they are. You may notice their friendships changing, and they may settle in to a completely new group of friends that doesn't include any of their primary school friends quite soon after starting secondary school.'

- They like some time to themselves, perhaps reading or playing on the computer.

Some children are naturally extroverted and brimming with confidence. If your child fits the description below, you should encourage them to join school clubs and extra-curricular activities – this way, they will be socialising with a wide range of other children rather than their usual group of friends.

- They might thrive on interaction with other children and become very energetic in social situations.

- They may constantly want to talk, becoming bored and unhappy when they're on their own.

- They might enjoy team games and competitive sports.

You have been involved in your child's friendships for their whole life. Not a great deal changes at secondary school, except you might feel more distanced from the situation. You definitely won't be meeting them at the school gate and talking to the parents of your child's friends. So if you want to know who your child is friendly with – and the sort of influence their friends might have over them – then get involved and be proactive.

- Encourage your child to invite friends round for tea or at a weekend.

- Arrange outings where they can bring a friend along.

- Give them some privacy – they are growing up and may not want a parent listening in on their chat all the time.

- Be aware of what they watch on TV or DVD – different parents have different values. You might not mind if your children watch 15- or 18-rated films, but their friends' parents might.

Helping your child make friends

Shyness usually stems from a lack of self-esteem. Most children start to feel very self-conscious at around 11 or 12 years old, as they reach puberty. If you have a shy child, it is vital that you make them feel good about themselves. You could make a special effort to praise them and boost their confidence.

- Pay your child regular compliments, e.g. for making an effort with some difficult homework, regardless of whether they get top marks for it.

- Encourage your child to socialise with other shy children or join lunchtime clubs where they may meet like-minded individuals.

- Encourage them to take up a hobby, perhaps a musical instrument or a sport.

- If your child becomes very unhappy, you could speak to their form tutor – they may be able to devise ways to get your child to interact more with the other children.

Bullying

No parent wants their child to be bullied, and no parent wants their child to be a bully. Bullies often suffer from low self-esteem, just like their victims, and they bully to gain confidence by being the one in control, sometimes starting out as the victim's friend.

How to recognise if your child is being bullied

Children who are bullied may not tell their parents or teachers, often because they feel they have in some way invited the bullying or that they will be bullied even more once they reveal what is happening. If you're worried about your child being bullied, signs to look out for are:

- Unexplained bruises or signs of a fight, e.g. ripped clothing.

- Your child not wanting to go to school and possibly even taking unauthorised absences.

- Sullen and uncommunicative moods, withdrawing from usual activities.

- Lack of eye contact and a negative attitude about themselves.

- Being depressed and more clingy than usual.

- Not using their computer or mobile phone.

- Taking a different route to school – or not wanting to get the school bus.

'Bullies often suffer from low self-esteem, just like their victims, and they bully to gain confidence by being the one in control, sometimes starting out as the victim's friend.'

- Suffering from nightmares and panic attacks.

It is important that your child can confide in you, so if you see any of these signs, you should speak to your child about what is happening. Think about what you want to say and choose a time when you will not be interrupted. Stress that it is not their fault that they're being bullied and try to find out exactly what's been happening.

Involving the school

Schools must have a policy on bullying by law; it should clearly state what their response will be to the bullying and what their responsibilities are regarding the children involved. If you discover that your child is being bullied, you should:

- Find out what the school's policy is on bullying.

- Make an appointment to see your child's form tutor or head of year.

- Bring some evidence of the bullying, e.g. a belonging that has been defaced or damaged.

- Take notes of what is said throughout the meeting so you can look back at them later.

- Ask for a follow-up meeting so you and your child's school can review the situation.

'Try to build your child's self-confidence up and encourage them to build and maintain friendships outside of school.'

At home

Try to build your child's self-confidence up and encourage them to build and maintain friendships outside of school. Perhaps self-defence classes or something similar could help them to feel more confident. Other things that can help are:

- Doing fun things together.

- Treating your child like an adult to show that you respect and trust them.

- Teach your child good posture; walking tall helps you to feel and look more confident.

For more information on bullying and how you can help your child, see *Bullying – A Parent's Guide* (Need2Know).

Boyfriends and girlfriends – future issues

Secondary school and puberty inevitably means relationships will be an issue most parents will have to think about at some point. Often the media can enforce the view that having a boyfriend or girlfriend is a desirable situation for teenagers, and sexual relationships, STIs and teenage pregnancy are all risks of this behaviour. You can help your child by:

- Being open with your child and encouraging them to be open with you.

- Encouraging them to have a wide circle of friends of both sexes. Don't let them believe that boys or girls who are friends have to be boyfriends or girlfriends in a romantic sense.

- Establishing boundaries that you feel comfortable with. If you're not happy about boyfriends or girlfriends staying overnight then say so.

- Discussing the issues of contraception, pregnancy and STIs with your child. It might be a little awkward but much better to prevent these things from happening than deal with them once they have happened.

- Bearing in mind that peer pressure can be very powerful, many children find it easier to say 'My parents won't allow it', rather than admit they don't want to participate, so don't be afraid of saying no to something you're not comfortable with.

As a parent all you can do is offer some guidance, and not be too dictatorial which often makes matters worse. For more information on issues surrounding teenage relationships, please see *Sexually Transmitted Infections – The Essential Guide* (Need2Know) and *Teenage Pregnancy – The Essential Guide* (Need2Know).

Smoking, alcohol and drugs

The dangers of smoking, alcohol and drugs become more apparent when your child begins mixing with lots of other children, many of whom you will not know. Their parents may have different values to yours and you may feel that you no longer have the same control over what your child does.

Your child's school will have a policy on smoking, alcohol and drugs. Regardless of what your own views are, the law states very clearly that there are age limits for smoking and drinking and which drugs are illegal. Many schools will expel children who repeatedly abuse drugs. If you suspect that your child is becoming involved with alcohol and drugs, you should:

- Speak with your child regularly, find out what's going on in their world and maintain an honest relationship between yourselves.

- Remember that during your child's teenage years it is normal for them to be moody or tired, so try not to jump to conclusions straightaway that they're experimenting with drugs or drinking all the time.

- Be open about alcohol and drugs, the dangers they present to your child's physical health and the legal implications of being caught.

- Keep on building your child's self-esteem. If they feel happy and confident in themselves, they will be more likely to refuse to take part in situations they don't feel comfortable in.

- Remember, you can't live your child's life for them. Some pushing of the boundaries is to be expected throughout the teenage years, but by being supportive and open you can help your child through any issues that might come up.

For more information on drugs, please see *Drugs – A Parent's Guide* (Need2Know).

What is acceptable to other parents?

As your child gets older and starts going to parties, sleepovers or has friends at home, they might be watching TV, DVDs, using the Internet and possibly drinking alcohol. It is worth remembering that all families have their own ideas on what is acceptable at certain ages.

If you child is offered alcohol at a friend's home, are you happy about that? Similarly, if you allow your child completely free access to the Internet or TV, do you know what they are accessing – and do their friends' parents? It is always worth talking to your child about this if it worries you.

Summing Up

■ Be prepared for your child to make new friends, and encourage them to socialise and take part in extra-curricular activities and other hobbies.

■ Build up your child's confidence and self-esteem by praising them for their efforts and encouraging them in any new activities they take up.

■ Look out for the signs of bullying and take the appropriate action.

■ Discuss the issues surrounding relationships, smoking, alcohol and drugs openly with your child.

Chapter Six

Common Problems

Your child's experience at secondary school is a journey. Sometimes that journey will be smooth and problem-free – like a steady drive on a quiet motorway, but at other times it can be a frustrating journey along winding country roads or a busy city centre. Your role is to help them navigate that journey while allowing them to be independent and build confidence.

Tricky teachers

Teachers are only human. They do not set out to make enemies of their pupils or their parents, but occasionally things do go wrong.

A common moan from children is 'My teacher always picks on me'. What they mean is that their teacher lays the blame for bad behaviour on them. Sometimes this is unjustified, but sometimes it's not. Whichever it is, your child can end up unhappy, and even begin skipping lessons.

So, what can be done and how do you get at the truth?

First, admit that your child is not an angel and the teacher is not an ogre. The truth usually lies somewhere in the middle. When writing this book, I did a lot of research and asked lots of teachers what they thought about the 'picking' complaint. They all said that they never pick on a child without good reason. What often happens is children misbehave as a group, they pass notes around the class, throw things around the room, kick each other under the desk and more. One child starts this and the others join in, some children are very good at starting bad behaviour and never being caught out. Others aren't. It might be that your child is the last to join in with the mucking about, but the first one to be spotted. So they will be challenged by the teacher and punished. It's not right and it's not fair – but it does happen.

What can you do? As always, communication is best. You can write to or email the teacher and explain how your child feels, or you can request a meeting to clear the air. Do not paint your child as whiter than white, and do not be confrontational. Agree to work together to help sort out the situation.

It might happen that your child is given low grades for their work, which seems unjustified. For instance, your child is given a grade D for a piece of work that is almost identical to their friend's – yet the friend is awarded a grade C.

If this happens regularly, speak to the teacher. It could be that your child's work is not as good as they think in which case the grade is accurate. However, it does occasionally happen that a teacher grades down, rather than up, if a piece of work is borderline. If this happens regularly and the situation doesn't change, your child might become frustrated and demoralised. You could make an appointment to see the teacher and discuss with them what might be done to help your child.

My child is in the wrong set

If your child's school uses setting (placing pupils of similar ability together), you may or may not be told by the school which set your child is placed in. It could be the case that the school inform you as part of their report, at parents' evening, or by assuming that your child will tell you.

Some schools set straightaway – possibly using KS2 SATs scores as a guide. They might set in all subjects or just some. Classes may be mixed ability in Year 7 and then exams will decide sets for Year 8.

The most usual reasons for children being in the wrong set are:

- They find the work is too easy.

- They find the work is too hard.

- There is a personality clash with the teacher.

- They are distracted by others' bad behaviour.

- They are picked-on or bullied by other pupils.

Only intervene if your child becomes very unhappy, or if you feel their education is suffering because of the set they are in.

All schools have a different approach to setting: some are happy to move pupils between sets at any time of the school year, others prefer to wait until September or at least until the start of a term. One factor which can prevent easy movement between sets is pupil numbers – if a set is full, then a pupil can only be moved up if another pupil is moved down.

The most common complaint from parents is that the work is too easy and their child is coasting. Some parents think it would be better for their child to be at the bottom of the top set, rather than the top of the middle or bottom sets. You know your child best. If your child has a problem with confidence, they may feel happier in a middle set, rather than at the bottom of the top set. If your child is bright but lazy, they might respond positively to working alongside other bright, motivated pupils in a high set. These are all the issues to discuss with the teacher.

Occasionally, there may be a clash of personality with a teacher, having got off to a bad start for some reason. It shouldn't happen, but it can. Your child might be put in a set with some disruptive students who may distract them regularly, and this might result in reduced concentration and work that is below their usual standard. Similarly, your child might be in a set with their worst enemy who makes life difficult for them at every opportunity. Or worse, they might be subject to bullying.

These are all valid reasons for moving sets. Follow the steps for communicating with the school:

- Speak to your child's subject teacher, outlining the problem. You could phone, email or write to them at this stage requesting a meeting.

- Discuss the problem and be prepared to listen to the teacher – you might not have the full story from your child!

- Agree on an outcome or a date to speak again.

'Only intervene if your child becomes very unhappy, or if you feel their education is suffering because of the set they are in.'

Communication with the school

Once your child starts secondary school, you will feel more removed from proceedings than you did when they were at primary school. You may have to rely on your child to give you letters or messages – but children can forget. Don't rummage in your child's bag – it might be the solution in the short term, but it won't change their behaviour longer term. Neither will it develop feelings of respect – would you like it if they ransacked your bag? So how can you ensure you find those all-important missives from school?

- Develop a routine where you ask for letters on a certain day of the week.

- Have a special place for letters from school, such as an 'in tray'. This will encourage your child to be independent.

- Respect your child's privacy – don't dig into their bag.

Most schools have websites where they have a calendar of important dates. This way you can put parents' nights into your diary, along with all the other important dates. However, as not all parents have computers at home or access to them at work, there will be alternative ways of accessing the information, most probably via a letter that your child brings home.

Contacting teachers

It's all about finding a balance when you are considering contacting a teacher about a particular issue. If you become really concerned, check when the next parents' night is coming up. If it is not for several weeks, or even months, you may need to act sooner – try not to let situations drift when a quick meeting or phone call might sort it out.

Remember – you will only have about 5-10 minutes at parents' night to speak with a teacher, so this isn't time to have an in-depth discussion on something important. Teachers don't usually mind if parents contact them, but keep a sense of perspective on the situation – if it's a minor issue, try not to be over-anxious or too fussy. Equally, don't be afraid of approaching your child's teacher if the issue is affecting your child's happiness and has not so far been resolved by other means.

Catching up on missed work

Most children lose a few days from school now and then. If this happens, make sure that your child does all they can to catch-up. They can:

- Ask the teacher for any hand outs they have missed.
- Borrow a friend's notes to copy out the missed work.
- Ask their teacher for some extra help to catch up.

This is very important if your child is in Year 10 or 11. They definitely need to catch-up as it is more than likely that the work will not be repeated until they do some revision much nearer to the exams.

Lost equipment and PE kits

Lost belongings drive parents and teachers to distraction. If your child has to borrow every pen, pencil or compass they need, then that's a distraction for their friends too. Make sure your child is organised and has all of the equipment they need for their lessons. A trip to the stationers every now and then is a good way to bring all equipment up-to-date.

- Colour code your child's timetable and pin it up in their room. Colour in all the lessons where they need extra equipment – whether that's sports kit or art equipment. That way, they can easily spot the days when they need to pack their kit. Encourage your child to do this for themselves as they get older.

- With younger children – Years 7 and 8 – encourage them to do a pencil case check each week. Replace anything that's lost or broken, or better still, give them the money and ask them to buy it – this will encourage responsibility.

- Put a spare pen and pencil in their rucksack or pocket, so if all else fails they will at least have the basics.

- Make sure all clothing is named, that way it should be easily identifiable.

- You or your child should follow up on lost kit. The lost property box is usually overflowing at the end of term and you'd be surprised how much of it is named!

'Lost belongings drive parents and teachers to distraction. If your child has to borrow every pen, pencil or compass they need, then that's a distraction for their friends too.'

Summing Up

- Maintain communication with the school. If your child develops problems because they're in the wrong set or the home situation changes, be open and honest with your child's teachers.

- Find a good routine for receiving information from the school, perhaps checking the website or reminding your child to pass on newsletters.

- Make sure your child has the correct equipment and kit for their lessons. Name all items of clothing and follow up on lost kit. Encourage them to check this for themselves as they get older.

Chapter Seven

Communicating Effectively with the School

There are two main ways to be in contact with the school: parents' evenings and other meetings with the teachers.

Parents' evening

Parents' evening planning begins when your child brings home a letter from the school inviting you. You won't just be meeting one teacher, but possibly as many as seven or eight. In addition, you will have to be in the right place at the right time – and your child may or may not be with you. The time spent with each teacher will be between 5-10 minutes, so you should try to maximise what is covered. However, this meeting is there to give you an update and a snap shot of your child's progress – it is not the time for in-depth discussions on certain issues.

Some parents feel unsure of how to handle these meetings. You might feel slightly intimidated if the teacher uses lots of jargon which you don't understand; you might find it hard to raise the points that bother you, and often parents can come away feeling that they haven't found out what they really wanted to know.

It is always helpful to plan ahead, so try to rearrange work or other commitments in advance so you can attend the parents' evening. Also, arranging childcare for other children you may have is a good idea, that way distractions are kept to a minimum.

What will be discussed?

Many teachers I have spoken to say that parents often raise issues that require more time than is available at parents' evening, e.g. friendships, bullying, long-term problems with motivation or homework issues. From a teacher's point of view, they would much rather you made a separate appointment to discuss these important issues – and not save them up for parents' evening – where time is limited to a 5-10 minute slot.

As a parent you may feel frustrated at the small amount of time you have with each teacher and come away feeling you have not achieved very much. To help make the most of the short amount of time with each teachers, you should make some notes about what you want to speak about to each teacher. Think about all the main topics, such as academic performance, friendships, motivation, confidence and anything that worries you in particular about your child. If you feel you need more time to discuss a particular issue, ask the teacher if you can make an appointment to see them at another time.

'Many teachers I have spoken to say that parents often raise issues that require more time than is available at parents' evening.'

Understanding the jargon

If you have not been into a secondary school since you left, then you could find the language used has changed. Don't worry about admitting that you don't understand something – teachers become so used to talking in jargon, especially when it comes to levels of achievement, that they often forget that parents don't understand.

School and home is a partnership, with your child's progress at its heart. Parents' evenings are there to iron out any problems before they become bigger problems, and for you to find out more about your child's progress.

Other issues

There are often occasions during any child's education when you will feel the need to communicate with school. Some of these occasions may be emotive – for instance if your child has been treated unfairly in your opinion, if they have been bullied, or if you are unhappy with the teaching.

It is tempting and understandable to want to make contact straightaway and say how you feel; however, this may not be the best way to resolve the situation. One thing that teachers hate is to be caught unawares by parents who either turn up at school or telephone them without warning. It can be very hard to pin down a teacher on the phone – they are either teaching or having a well-earned break for a few minutes. If you do need to talk to them, it is better to arrange a good time for both of you.

When should you step in?

In as many instances as possible, encourage your child to take responsibility for the issues. This will help develop their confidence. Encourage them to find the teacher they need to talk to and discuss whatever is bothering them.

Changes at home

It is vital that school is kept in the picture if there are any changes at home that might affect your child's learning. This can be anything from the family pet dying, to moving house, to separation or divorce. You might feel uneasy about contacting school, especially if you are feeling very emotional, but it will be useful for the school to know in case of changes in your child's behaviour or quality of work.

- They might lose interest in their schoolwork because they are preoccupied with their home situation.

- They might vent their anger and frustration about a home situation by picking fights.

- There could be topics covered in lessons that they will find upsetting.

If their teacher knows what is going on outside of school, they can make any necessary allowances and even offer support.

'It is vital that school is kept in the picture if there are any changes at home that might affect your child's learning. This can be anything from the family pet dying, to moving house, to separation or divorce.'

Who to contact

As a rough guide your points of contact should be as follows:

- Form tutor for general problems or queries, e.g. absences; essential appointments such as doctor appointment; missing or stolen equipment.

- Subject teachers for anything to do with a particular lesson, e.g. problems with homework; queries over coursework.

- Head of year for more serious problems, e.g. bullying; changes at home such as parent's separating.

- Head teacher for very important issues, e.g. bullying; being in trouble out of school for something; refusing to go to school.

Summing Up

- Make the most of parents' evenings, rearrange other commitments and organise childcare to ensure you can attend with no distractions.

- Make notes about anything you'd like to bring up with particular teachers, that way you won't forget and kick yourself when the appointment's over.

- Don't use parents' evening for discussing serious issues regarding your child, make a separate appointment to ensure any concerns can be addressed properly.

- Ask the teachers to explain any jargon they use if you do not understand.

Chapter Eight

The Curriculum, GCSEs, AS and A Levels

The curriculum

No doubt the curriculum and exam system now used at school has changed since you were there yourself. For a better understanding, the following subjects are compulsory in Years 7-9.

- Art and design – pupils will be able to experiment with a range of materials, learn about shape and form, as well as explore the differences between other forms of art, e.g. sculpture and photography.

- Citizenship – this includes discussions on rights, responsibilities, law, freedom and democracy.

- Design and technology – this can include graphic design, electronics, resistant materials, textiles and food technology.

- English – pupils are encouraged to develop speaking, listening, writing and reading skills. This subject will be similar to what you studied as a child.

- Maths – children are taught how to apply and communicate mathematics and how to select the correct tools and methods to solve problems.

- Science – this will include elements of biology, chemistry and physics, either combined in one subject or as three separate subjects. Your child will learn through practical experiments as well as by textbooks.

- Geography – this will teach your child about the structure of the earth, how people and the environment interact, a country's economics, natural resources and the lives of people across different continents.

- History – this covers early and modern civilizations, in Britain, Europe and the world, and how the past influences our present and future.

- Information and communications technology (ICT) – your child will learn how to use computers and may also study the subject itself at GCSE.

- Modern foreign languages – these are French, German, Spanish and possibly Italian. All children will study at least one, or possibly two, languages in Years 7 and 8.

- Music – this will instill an appreciation of music in your child as well as giving them the chance to perform, either in a choir, orchestra or by learning an instrument, as well as learning about music throughout the world and throughout the centuries.

- PE – your child will be able to learn about and participate in sports.

- Careers – this will teach your child about employment prospects for when they leave school.

- Personal health and social education (PHSE) – this covers many topics including religion, sex education, drugs, alcohol, personal relationships and finances.

- Religious education (RE) – this subject covers different religions around the world as well as sometimes discussion of ethical and moral issues.

If you would like more in-depth information on the curriculum and the subjects listed above, see www.qcda.gov.uk.

In Years 10 and 11, the compulsory subjects are:

- English.

- Maths.

- Science.

- ICT.

- PE.

- Citizenship.
- Careers.
- PHSE.
- RE.

KS3 SATs

KS3 SATs in English, maths and science used to be taken at the end of Year 9. Although these exams are not compulsory any more, some schools ask their pupils to take similar end of year tests as a means of measuring their progress.

GCSEs

GCSEs are graded from A*-G. If your child needs particular GCSEs in order to start a course following school, they will be asked for grades A*-C.

Grades D and lower are not considered pass grades. Grade U stands for unclassified and no qualification is awarded.

GCSE subjects

You can see that in Years 10 and 11 your child will be studying fewer compulsory subjects. However, they will make up the rest of their subjects by choosing from the other subjects they studied in Years 7-9. Most children study between seven and 11 GCSE subjects.

In some subjects there are different levels of exams that your child can be entered for or awards that can be awarded. In maths and English there are foundation and higher tiers, and in science, single, double and triple awards. Your child's subject teacher will make the decision about which level is appropriate based on a combination of exam or test results, grades for work done in class, attitude and ability. There may be room for discussion on this with you, your child and the teacher if you do not agree with the teacher's decision.

The idea behind this is that children can be taught at the level best suited to their ability. However, there is a ceiling to the grades awarded within each tier; foundation level can only be awarded C-G grade, and higher level A*-D grade. For science the award is indicative of the amount of time spent studying the subject – the single award is worth one GCSE, the double award is two GCSEs and the triple award is three GCSEs. The triple award is where biology, chemistry and physics are studied separately.

This is important because if your child wants to continue to A Level science, they will need to have studied double science at GCSE at least. It would be impossible for a child who had studied for a single science award to proceed to A Level science, because they would not have enough in-depth knowledge as the basis for the A Level.

Choosing the subjects to study

Somewhere towards the end of Year 9 your child will be asked to decide which GCSE subjects they'd like to take. As you'll see from the previous list, some subjects are compulsory. In Years 10 and 11 some subjects are not studied anymore and one or two others, which might not have been on the timetable already, are. At this stage, your child can also decide not to continue studying a foreign language.

It is impossible to cover here all the possible subjects that might be on offer, but how you should choose is the same. As a rule, your child should choose the subjects they are most interested in and in which they have a chance of obtaining good grades. They also need to think about which subjects they might follow through to at A Level. It is possible even at this early stage to close doors in terms of career prospects, simply by not choosing the best GCSE subjects. Another thing to consider is the amount of coursework involved in a subject.

Coursework

When your child reaches the stage of looking at GCSE choices, make sure you find out what the GCSE course involves – this is something that teachers should be willing to discuss with you. Some courses include a lot of coursework, which has its advantages and disadvantages.

High coursework content

- Advantages – there will be fewer exams, ongoing feedback can boost confidence, and the learning and testing on these courses is in smaller chunks.

- Disadvantages – children have to work steadily and be self-motivated, so this may not be suited to children who like to cram before exams and who work best under pressure.

Low coursework content

- Advantages – suited to children who work well under pressure and in exams, the course does not require consistent effort over many months.

- Disadvantages – requires a good memory for exams and can be hard for children who get very nervous, and whose performance varies from day to day.

The school should inform you of the coursework content for each subject, but if you are in any doubt, or don't fully understand, ask the teacher or ask your child to find out and bring the information home.

AS Level and A Level

Advanced Subsidiary Level (AS Level) and Advanced Level (A Level) are the next step up from GCSE. A Level is sometimes called A2. Most children choose between three and five AS Levels to study in Year 12. They will continue with three or four of these in Year 13. Rarely, they will continue with five.

A Levels and AS Levels are worth a certain number of points, depending on the grade achieved. See the table overleaf.

Grade	A Level	AS Level
Grade A	120 points	60 points
Grade B	100 points	50 points
Grade C	80 points	40 points
Grade D	60 points	30 points
Grade E	40 points	20 points

'If your child is aiming for university, it is very important that they find out well in advance which subjects are required for the various degree courses.'

What's the point of points?

Some universities allocate places according to grades at AS and A Level, others work on a points system. The advantage of the points system is that all AS and A2 grades can be added together. However, most of the top universities insist on certain grades, rather than allowing candidates to accumulate points from a wide range of AS and A2 exams.

Choosing the right A Levels

The time to think about A Level subjects is when your child decides on their GCSE subjects and possibly after they receive their grades for those exams. This is because, with a few exceptions, most subjects at A Level are a progression from GCSE level. For instance, if your child wants to study art at A Level, they will have to study it for GCSE.

Many schools insist that a pupil has achieved at least a grade B at GCSE in order to study it at AS or A Level. If your child obtains a lower grade at GCSE than the school accepts as a basis for A Level study – such as a grade B when your the school requires a grade A – then you can negotiate with them, especially if your child needs that subject for university.

A Levels and university

If your child is aiming for university, it is very important that they find out in advance which subjects are required for the various degree courses. All this information should be found on the university website or in their prospectus which can be requested at any time. You need to obtain this information before the start of Year 12.

Avoiding the 'soft subject' trap

Over recent years, universities have become more selective about A Level subjects, mainly in response to the popularity of certain subjects that are not considered as academic. Do not assume that any subject will be acceptable.

General studies, media studies, business studies, design and technology, tourism, possibly psychology and other vocational subjects can sometimes be seen as 'soft subjects'.

In other words, these subjects are considered not as academically demanding as pure sciences, maths or languages. So if your child applies for a very popular degree course, this is relevant. Very few of the top universities accept general studies A Level, so make sure your child chooses carefully.

It might seem ridiculous that your child has to think about university when they have not even taken their GCSEs but, because of how the system works, it's advisable! It's not something they should leave to chance, and leaving it until they are halfway through Year 12 is too late.

'Children who do not want to follow an academic route will find many vocational courses on offer at colleges of further education.'

Vocational qualifications, apprenticeships and employment

Children who do not want to follow an academic route will find many vocational courses on offer at colleges of further education. These will include subjects in the following fields:

- Accounting and book keeping.

- Motor vehicle.

- Health and beauty.
- IT.
- Childcare.
- Plumbing.

Many apprenticeships include day-release to study at college as well as learning the practical side of the work in employment. For more information, check your local college's prospectus or website.

Alternatively, employment is another option and many employers will help your child gain further qualifications through a college or their own training schemes. It's a good idea to research companies to see what is on offer for school leavers and the training schemes offered.

Summing Up

- Try to help your child when they choose their GCSE subjects in Year 9. They should think about what they'd like to study in Years 12 and 13 when making the choices.

- Bear in mind what universities will look for when your child chooses their AS and A Level subjects.

- If your child does not want to stay on at school for A Levels, look at colleges, apprenticeships and employment.

- Obtain prospectuses from your local colleges and visit them on open days if your child is interested in a vocational course.

- If you child wants to go straight into employment it's worth looking at different companies and what schemes they may have in place for school leavers.

Chapter Nine

Revision and Motivation

Parental support can make a huge difference to a child's achievements. It doesn't matter whether your child is preparing for SATs, GCSEs or A Levels – the same rules apply.

Some children get very worried as exams approach. You can help by being positive, getting actively involved in the revision and not allowing them to be defeatist if they are struggling. As with all goals, they need to keep the long-term goal in mind – so remind them of the goals they are working towards. At the same time, reassure your child that if they don't succeed this time around, they can try again and that there is more than one route to any destination.

Don't allow your own negative experiences to affect their progress. For instance, you might feel like saying, 'Well, I wasn't any good at maths, but it didn't do me any harm' or even, 'You are just like me – hopeless at maths'. Just think of the negative message this sends out. Consider how much better it is to say, 'I wish I'd worked hard at maths, I'm sure I could be good at it' or 'You are good at maths, everyone finds some bits of it tricky'.

How does your child learn best?

Everyone has a way of remembering information, and different ways suit different people. Some of us learn in a visual way – by reading and looking at words and diagrams – some of us learn best by listening, and some of us learn best with a hands-on approach, by putting what we learn into practice.

Ask your child to analyse how they learn best.

- Visual learners like reading, making notes and inventing memory-jogging diagrams.
- Auditory learners like listening to information or reading aloud.

- Hands-on, or kinesthetic learners, learn by doing and being actively involved.

Often, learning involves all of these. If your child prefers one way, then try to make the most of that. For example, if they are a visual learner, written information can be turned into diagrams, graphs and bite sized information on postcards. Auditory learners can read their notes onto a tape recorder and listen to it whenever possible. Hands-on learners can get the most out of their revision by doing some questions and exercises, instead of just reading notes or textbooks.

'Break revision into small chunks. Most of us cannot concentrate fully for more than 20 or 30 minutes, so don't expect your child to revise for hours without a break.'

How to plan revision

Revision should be broken into small chunks. Most of us cannot concentrate fully for more than 20 or 30 minutes, so don't expect your child to revise for hours without a break. Suggest they make a revision plan, as shown here:

- Break the week into seven days, then morning, afternoon and evening.
- Block out any regular commitments.
- Block out times for lunch and dinner.
- Decide how much time each week is going to be spent on each subject – some will require more revision than others.

It is a good idea to revise a subject on the same day they have that lesson at school. So if they have science on Mondays and Thursdays, schedule science revision on those days. With the remaining times left, after their commitments and eating has been timetabled, allocate half an hour to a subject with a 15 minute break after it. Be realistic, if they arrive home at 4.30pm, they will need half an hour at least to have a snack and relax before they get down to work. The amount of time your child spends on homework will, of course, depend on their age, amount set and what time they go to bed.

A typical evening's revision for GCSE or A Level exams might look like this:

Start time	Finish time	Activity
4.30pm	5pm	Arrive home from school, have a snack and relax
5.00pm	5.30pm	Science revision
5.30pm	5.45pm	Break
5.45pm	6.30pm	Science revision
6.30pm	7.00pm	Eat dinner
7.00pm	7.30pm	French revision
7.30pm	7.45pm	Break
7.45pm	8.30pm	English revision
8.30pm	9.00pm	Break
9.00pm	9.30pm	Maths revision
9.30pm		Relax before going to bed

Information is stored better by learning little and often, e.g. three bursts of 30 minutes produces better results than one stint of two hours. Make sure that learning is active, as reading pages and pages of notes may not be enough. Information might be remembered better if it were broken down into a few bullet points on a postcard. Tricky formulae and equations can be posted on a pin board, so it's there as a constant visual reminder.

- Be supportive and optimistic, try not to allow any negative thinking. If your child constantly moans that they 'can't learn this…', replace that with a 'you can…let's see what we can do together'.

- Break down learning into small chunks – 20-30 minutes then a break of 10 minutes is better than an hour without a break.

- Create a quiet part of the house where your child can revise undisturbed. Ideally this will be their own room, with a desk and so on, but if this isn't possible, at least provide a table on which they can work. Try to make sure other children are considerate and keep the noise down.

- A pin board is always helpful for sticking up messages, reminders and timetables.

- Make allowances for short fuses. Children who are stressed may behave badly, or even withdraw. Notice the signs and adapt your responses. Temper outbursts might be a way of releasing tension or frustration, so don't respond angrily – ask if they need some help with their revision, or if there is anything you can do.

- Provide nutritious food and drink. The brain is 75% water, so make sure they have water on hand, or offer drinks. Avoid buying junk food and fizzy sugary drinks, as these give a short burst of energy followed by a low. They can also make some children unable to concentrate.

- Be willing to give your time – actively help with revision, by testing them for example.

- Think carefully about social arrangements that might clash with, or come immediately before, a big exam.

- Don't nag. Try to avoid reminding your child every day about their revision, especially older children. If you are really worried about their motivation, it is better to raise the issue when you are calm and have time to chat about things, rather than nagging them every day. You can encourage them and be supportive, but you cannot make them revise if they simply don't want to.

'Provide nutritious food and drink. The brain is 75% water, so make sure they have water on hand, or offer drinks. Avoid buying junk food and fizzy sugary drinks, as these give a short burst of energy followed by a low. They can also make some children unable to concentrate.'

74

Books, revision guides and past exam papers

Books

When the time comes, there are simply masses of publications that you can buy to help at home. Most are available from bookshops or online book suppliers. A word of caution – before you rush out, find out which syllabus your child is studying. This is not so relevant for SATs but it is absolutely essential for GCSEs and A Levels. If you're not sure about anything, contact your child's school. Some schools publish this information for parents, and some don't, but you can easily find out.

Revision guides

There are masses of revision guides available. Some are excellent and others are not. For AS and A Level revision, it is best to ask the school what they recommend – in fact many schools will supply revision guides for you to buy. If you have to buy your own, then most bookshops stock them, and online companies like Amazon too; one advantage to shopping online is that you can read other students' reviews of the books. It's also possible to pick them up cheaply from online sites such as Ebay.

For GCSE and KS3 SATs much comes down to personal choice. Let your child choose their own: the layout of these books are very different and appeal to different people – some are highly visual, with lots of diagrams and colours, which some children like but which others find confusing.

Revision guides which contain questions and answers are great, because then your child can really monitor their progress.

Past exam papers

Most of the examination boards allow you to buy old exam papers. Find out the exam board, the syllabus and any variations on the syllabus before you buy. In most cases, you have to order by phone or online. Schools often allow pupils to use their supply of old papers, or work through them in lessons, but if you want any more – or need them sooner – buy your own. They cost around £2-3 a paper.

See *How to Pass Exams – A Parent's Guide* (Need2Know) for more information on helping your child through their revision.

Motivation

There is nothing so frustrating for a parent as watching their child not putting effort into their studying and as a result not achieving their best. It is so easy to nag, but it rarely brings results.

Often, lack of motivation is the result of a lack of confidence. Children can get into a spiral of failure. The fear of failure, or the experience of what is perceived as failure, can overwhelm some children, so they simply stop trying.

How does this happen? Perhaps there is a series of poor results in tests; difficulty in grasping a concept or a new topic; falling behind with coursework; not getting on with a particular teacher; or the influence of peers who regard success at school as 'geeky' or 'un-cool'.

What can you do to help? First, try to understand what is holding your child back – is it friends, failure, volume of work, disorganisation – or something else? Once you understand what you are dealing with, then you can help to put it right.

Sometimes a 'hands-off' approach works better, sometimes talking seriously about their attitude once in a while works better than daily nagging. You know your child best, so try to work out what approach is most effective.

Summing Up

- Help your child stay positive about their learning, be encouraging and supportive.

- Work out your child's learning style and create revision aids based on their preferences.

- Encourage your child to plan revision sessions and make sure they take plenty of breaks.

- Make sure your child eats and drinks the right kind of food and drink during revision and in the run up to exams.

- Use books, revision guides and past exam papers for extra resources.

- Help to maintain motivation by talking to your child about their revision.

Chapter Ten

Post-16 Options

At present, your child can legally leave school at 16, but from 2013 it will increase to 18. When your child leaves school, there are several options.

Post GSCE:

- A Levels at a secondary school, 6th form college or college of further education.

- International Baccalaureate.

- Vocational courses at a college of further education.

- Apprenticeship.

- Employment.

- Armed forces and police.

Post A Level:

- University.

- Employment and employment with further training.

- Armed forces and police.

- Gap year or voluntary work.

Post GCSE

A Levels

Following an A Level route suits young people who are academic, but there are also other courses available after GCSE which include a more practical, or coursework, element. It is worth pointing out that although some young people are ready to leave school after GCSEs, the slightly more adult environment of a college or a 6th form college can offer them an alternative to school. They will be encouraged to study more independently, which could suit them very well.

International Baccalaureate

This is taking the place of A Levels in some schools, mainly independent schools. It introduces pupils to a broader curriculum as they often study up to six subjects. It is a highly-regarded examination and is looked on favourably by universities.

Vocational courses

Vocational courses are available for people who do not want to follow the usual academic route. The emphasis of these courses is on practical learning and experience, with assessments carried out throughout the course. The most common types of vocational qualifications are NVQ (National Vocational Qualification), National Diploma and National Certificate. The types of courses that are available at colleges of further education can include:

- Beauty therapy.
- Graphic design.
- Health and social care.
- Photography.
- Travel and tourism.
- Childcare and education.
- Catering and hospitality.

■ Art and design.

Colleges have their own entry requirements; some will ask for four GCSEs at grade C and above, but it does vary. The best way to find out the entry requirements is to check the college's website or prospectus. Many colleges will also have open days or may even visit schools to distribute information leaflets on the courses they offer.

There are other courses available which tend to be at colleges specialising in certain subjects, for example:

■ Horticulture.

■ Animal care.

■ Veterinary nursing.

■ Agriculture.

■ Equine studies.

■ Countryside management.

Apprenticeship

Modern apprenticeships offer the chance to learn and be employed. Your child will need to be 16 or over to apply for an apprenticeship and the entry requirements will depend on the apprenticeship they want to do. There are three levels available:

■ Apprenticeship (equivalent to five good GCSE passes).

■ Advanced Apprenticeship (equivalent to two A Level passes).

■ Higher Apprenticeship (leads to qualifications at NVQ Level 4 or, in some cases, a Foundation Degree).

Depending on your child's grades in GCSE maths and English, they may need to take a literacy and numeracy test before being accepted on an apprenticeship scheme.

Apprenticeships can lead to:

■ An NVQ at Level 2 or 3.

- A Key Skills qualification, like problem solving and using technology.

- In most cases a technical certificate, such as a BTEC or City and Guilds Progression Award.

- Other qualifications needed for particular occupations.

Further information can be found on www.directgov.uk.

Employment

When your child reaches 16, they may feel ready to leave school. However, they should understand that employment opportunities are very limited for people with few qualifications, and this will become more noticeable when the school leaving age rises to 18. If they are able to have some further training as part of their employment if they leave at 16, they will have a much better chance of furthering their career in the years ahead. Some employers will allow a young person to study one day a week at a college in order to gain more skills and experience.

Armed forces and police

The armed forces can provide a worthwhile, secure career for many young people. They will possibly talk to your child's school at some point, but if not they will offer information and advice about the routes that are available. Entry into the armed forces can be at 16 or after graduation. There are many career paths in the armed forces, for more information visit www.army.mod.uk.

Everyone who wants to become a police officer must complete two years of working as a patrol constable, following this you can either remain as a patrol constable or transfer to a more specialist area of work undertaking the necessary training. The minimum age to join the police is 18 years old. There is no formal education requirement but written tests must be passed in order to join. If you have a criminal record, there are certain offences that could make you ineligible; however, if you have only minor convictions or cautions, you should still be eligible. A further requirement is that candidates must be physically and mentally fit enough to undertake the duties involved. For more information about joining the police, visit www.policecouldyou.co.uk.

For information on options for those not planning on going to university, visit www.notgoingtouni.co.uk.

Work experience placements

While your child is at school, they will usually undertake some work experience in Year 10. The aim of this is to give young people a taste of various types of employment. However, competition for placements amongst local organisations and companies can be high due to the pressure it places on those companies. It is possible, therefore, that your child's work experience placement may not link with their interests. Of course, they may also change their minds about what they would like to do for a career.

It is always worth considering whether your child can arrange their own work placement outside of the academic year with an organisation whose line of work they are interested in. This can even be an opening into employment in some cases.

Careers' advice

Schools can provide advice on careers, but the amount varies between schools. At some point during Year 11, and certainly Year 12 and 13, your child will most likely be contacted by Connexions which offer career information at a local level. Connexions have advisors which go into schools and they will also see your child on their own by appointment if they want further advice, especially if they are not going to continue down an academic route.

Post A Levels

University

If your child decides on a particular career path, then a university degree may be their best option. Although a degree can open many doors, it does not guarantee employment, especially now that the number of graduates has increased. Part of the discussion over what to study should of course include employment prospects. If your child wants to go to university then they need to start looking at courses and course requirements before they choose their A Level subjects.

For information on courses, universities and entry requirements, please see www.ucas.ac.uk. For information on applying for a university place, please see *Applying to University – The Essential Guide* (Need2Know).

Employment and employment with further training

Many large organisations will employ young people who have A Levels. Opportunities exist in retail, banking, insurance, accountancy and the public sectors. Often there will be the opportunity to obtain further training and qualifications. Your careers' office will be able to help your child find out about schemes in your area, as will the organisations themselves – websites should be checked regularly for jobs and information about training schemes.

Armed forces and police

Your child can join the armed forces or police at various levels, including post GCSE, post A Level and with a degree, with the armed forces this can help you to enter higher up the ranks or in a particular discipline, e.g. engineering, medical, etc. However, to enter the police your level of education doesn't mean you can enter higher up the ladder, every police officer must complete two years as a patrol constable and then take exams to progress up the rankings.

Candidates can also be sponsored in some instances by the armed forces whilst studying for a degree which will offset the cost of the degree. If you do this then you are obliged to join the armed forces for a minimum period of time. The armed forces' and police careers' departments will have details about this, and you can also check their websites and encourage your child to ask their careers advisor.

Gap year or volunteer scheme

If your child is undecided about what they want to do, or can defer entry to university, then a gap year might be helpful. However, be aware that unless it is constructive, it will not add anything to their employment prospects or their personal statement for university. If your child can take part in something that offers new skills and personal development, it will look better than if they spend time doing nothing but travelling.

There are all kinds of volunteer opportunities in the UK and abroad; for example, your child could choose from conservation work, teaching English as a foreign language and building projects. The list of activities that your child could volunteer to take part in is endless. They could also gain experience by taking paid work abroad, although it should be relevant to their long-term plans and could eventually give them an edge when seeking employment back in the UK.

Please see *Gap Years – The Essential Guide* (Need2Know) for information on taking a gap year.

Summing Up

- The school leaving age will rise from 16 to 18 in 2013.

- There are many routes available into employment after GCSEs and A Levels, think about what would suit your child, discuss the options with them and research the most appealing ones. University is not always right for everyone.

- Gap years and voluntary work are worthwhile if they are constructive and not simply time-fillers. Ask your child to think about how they would explain their time out of the country on their CV to a prospective employer.

Help List

Advisory Centre for Education (ACE Centre)

1c Aberdeen Studios, 22 Highbury Grove, London, N5 2DQ
Tel: 0808 800 5793 (helpline)
www.ace-ed.org.uk
Provides information about state education in England and Wales for children aged five to 16, with telephone advice on special educational needs matters.

Amazon

www.amazon.co.uk
Revision guides recommended by your child's school should be available from Amazon.

British Armed Forces

www.army.mod.uk
British armed forces' website with information on army careers.

British Dyslexia Association

Unit 8 Bracknell Beeches, Old Bracknell Lane, Bracknell, RG12 7BW
Tel: 0845 251 9002 (helpline)
helpline@bdadyslexia.org.uk
www.bdadyslexia.org.uk
Promotes support in schools to ensure opportunities to learn for dyslexic learners. It has lots of useful resources and touches on dyscalculia too.

Children's Legal Centre

www.childrenslegalcentre.com
The Children's Legal Centre provides free legal advice and assistance regarding school admissions through CLA Direct.

Connexions

www.connexions-direct.com
Information and advice for young people. You can search for your local service on the website.

Department for Education

www.education.gov.uk
Government department with responsibility for children, families and education. Previously called Department of Children, Schools and Families.

Direct Gov

www.direct.gov.uk
Official UK government website. Information on employment and education and training can be found on this site.

Dyslexia Action

Park House, Wick Road, Egham, Surrey, TW20 0HH
www.dyslexiaaction.org.uk
Dyslexia Action is a national charity and the UK's leading provider of services and support for people with dyslexia and literacy difficulties.

Dyspraxia Foundation

8 West Alley, Hitchin, Herts, SG5 1EG
Tel: 01462 454986 (helpline)
www.dyspraxiafoundation.org.uk
Organisation that seeks every opportunity to increase understanding of dyspraxia, particularly among professionals in health and education and encourages its local groups to do the same.

Ebay

www.ebay.co.uk
Revision guides recommended by your child's school may be available from Ebay at a cheaper price.

Independent Schools Council

www.isc.co.uk
Information on independent schools that belong to the Independent Schools Council.

Local Government Ombudsman

www.lgo.gov.uk
The Local Government Ombudsman looks at complaints about councils and some other authorities, including appeal panels. It is a free service.

Mumsnet

www.mumsnet.com
Website for parents offering discussion forums with other parents.

National Association for Gifted Children

Tel: 0845 450 0295
www.nagcbritain.org.uk
Information for parents of gifted and talented children.

National Autistic Society

Tel. 0845 070 4004
www.nas.org.uk
Information and support on autism, Asperger's syndrome and associated conditions.

National Bullying Helpline

Tel: 0845 22 55 787
www.nationalbullyinghelpline.co.uk
Charity dedicated to helping people affected by bullying.

Not Going to Uni

www.notgoingtouni.co.uk
Dedicated to helping young people make informed decisions about their future by showing the opportunities that exist outside of university.

Ofsted

Royal Exchange Buildings, St Ann's Square, Manchester, M2 7LA
enquiries@ofsted.gov.uk
www.ofsted.gov.uk
The body responsible for inspecting and regulating schools. Click on
'inspection reports' to view reports on schools throughout the UK.

Parentline Plus

Tel: 0808 800 2222 (helpline)
www.parentlineplus.org.uk
Charity providing help and support to anyone caring for children – parents,
grandparents, step-parents, relatives. For families living together as well as apart.

Police Could You?

www.policecouldyou.co.uk
Describes employment opportunities in police forces across the country, with
details of the lifestyle, pay and benefits, and application forms.

Qualifications and Curriculum Development Agency (QCDA)

53-55 Butts Road, Earlsdon Park, Coventry, CV1 3BH
info@qcda.gov.uk
www.qcda.gov.uk
The body responsible for developing the National Curriculum, improving and
delivering assessments, and reviewing and reforming qualifications.

School Appeals

www.schoolappeals.org.uk
Independent website offering advice on school appeals.

Special Educational Needs and Disability Tribunal Service (SENDIST)

www.sendist.gov.uk
SENDIST considers parents' appeals against the decisions of LAs about
children's special educational needs if parents cannot reach agreement with
the authority.

Talk to Frank

Tel: 0800 77 66 00 (helpline)
www.talktofrank.com
Information for people wanting to find out more about drugs and the risks of taking drugs. There is a 'worried about someone' section especially for family members.

UCAS

Tel: 0871 468 0 468
enquiries@ucas.ac.uk
www.ucas.com
UCAS is the UK central organisation through which applications are processed for entry to higher education. You can research courses using 'course search'. Make your application using 'apply' and follow the progress of your application using 'track'.

Book List

ADHD – The Essential Guide
By Diane Paul, Need2Know, Peterborough, 2008.

Applying to University – The Essential Guide
By Anne Coates, Need2Know, Peterborough, 2008.

Asperger's Syndrome – The Essential Guide
By Hilary Hawkes, Need2Know, Peterborough, 2009.

Autism – A Parent's Guide
By Hilary Hawkes, Need2Know, Peterborough, 2009.

Bullying – A Parent's Guide
By Jennifer Thomson, Need2Know, Peterborough, 2005.

Drugs – A Parent's Guide
By Judie Mackie, Need2Know, Peterborough, 2004.

Dyslexia and Other Learning Difficulties – A Parent's Guide
By Maria Chivers, Need2Know, Peterborough, 2004.

Gap Years – The Essential Guide
By Emma Jones, Need2Know, Peterborough, 2009.

The Good Schools Guide
By Ralph Lucas, Lucas Publications, London, 2010.

How to Pass Exams – A Parent's Guide
By David Lambourne, Need2Know, Peterborough, 2008.

Sexually Transmitted Infections – The Essential Guide
By Nicolette Heaton-Harris, Need2Know, Peterborough, 2008.

Special Educational Needs – A Parent's Guide
By Antonia Chitty and Victoria Dawson, Need2Know, Peterborough, 2008.

Teenage Pregnancy – The Essential Guide
By Nicolette Heaton-Harris, Need2Know, Peterborough, 2007.

Need - 2 - Know

Available Titles Include ...

Allergies A Parent's Guide
ISBN 978-1-86144-064-8 £8.99

Autism A Parent's Guide
ISBN 978-1-86144-069-3 £8.99

Drugs A Parent's Guide
ISBN 978-1-86144-043-3 £8.99

Dyslexia and Other Learning Difficulties
A Parent's Guide ISBN 978-1-86144-042-6 £8.99

Bullying A Parent's Guide
ISBN 978-1-86144-044-0 £8.99

Epilepsy The Essential Guide
ISBN 978-1-86144-063-1 £8.99

Teenage Pregnancy The Essential Guide
ISBN 978-1-86144-046-4 £8.99

Gap Years The Essential Guide
ISBN 978-1-86144-079-2 £8.99

How to Pass Exams A Parent's Guide
ISBN 978-1-86144-047-1 £8.99

Child Obesity A Parent's Guide
ISBN 978-1-86144-049-5 £8.99

Applying to University The Essential Guide
ISBN 978-1-86144-052-5 £8.99

ADHD The Essential Guide
ISBN 978-1-86144-060-0 £8.99

Student Cookbook - Healthy Eating The Essential Guide
ISBN 978-1-86144-061-7 £8.99

Stress The Essential Guide
ISBN 978-1-86144-054-9 £8.99

Adoption and Fostering A Parent's Guide
ISBN 978-1-86144-056-3 £8.99

Special Educational Needs A Parent's Guide
ISBN 978-1-86144-057-0 £8.99

The Pill An Essential Guide
ISBN 978-1-86144-058-7 £8.99

University A Survival Guide
ISBN 978-1-86144-072-3 £8.99

Diabetes The Essential Guide
ISBN 978-1-86144-059-4 £8.99

View the full range at **www.need2knowbooks.co.uk**. To order our titles, call **01733 898103**, email **sales@n2kbooks.com** or visit the website.

Need - 2 - Know, Remus House, Coltsfoot Drive, Peterborough, PE2 9JX